Just Give Me Jesus

JOURNAL

LEARNING TO LOVE GOD'S WORD

Just Give Me Jesus

JOURNAL

LEARNING TO LOVE GOD'S WORD

A 30-Day Journey through John's Gospel

ANNE GRAHAM LOTZ

W PUBLISHING GROUP™

www.wpublishinggroup.com

A Division of Thomas Nelson, Inc.
www.ThomasNelson.com

JUST GIVE ME JESUS JOURNAL: LEARNING TO LOVE GOD'S WORD

© 2003 Anne Graham Lotz. All rights reserved. No portion of this book may be reproduced, stored in a retrieval system, or transmitted in any form or by any means—electronic, mechanical, photocopy, recording, or any other—except for brief quotations in printed reviews, without the prior permission of the publisher.

Published by W Publishing Group, a Division of Thomas Nelson, Inc., P.O. Box 141000, Nashville, Tennessee 37214.

All Scripture quotations, unless otherwise indicated, are taken from The Holy Bible, New International Version (NIV). Copyright © 1973, 1978, 1984, International Bible Society. Used by permission of Zondervan Bible Publishers. The "NIV" and "New International Version" trademarks are registered in the United States Patent and Trademark Office by International Bible Society.

ISBN 0-8499-9045-9

Printed in the United States of America
03 04 05 06 07 PHX 9 8 7 6 5 4 3 2 1

Contents

Introduction to the Journey through John's Gospel 7

Getting Started 9

Tips for a Successful Journey 11

Completed Example 15

Day One through Day Thirty 19

"I am the living bread that came down from heaven.

If anyone eats of this bread, he will live forever."

JESUS CHRIST

Introduction
to
the Journey through John's Gospel

My beloved friend Jill Briscoe once visited what had been an extremely poverty-stricken country in Africa. As she flew in, she looked down on miles and miles of African veldt that had previously been covered by a lush grasslike crop, but was now an unbroken brown, dusty plain stretching all the way to the horizon. As Jill traveled to the mission station where she would be staying, mile after mile of barren, dry, poverty-stricken land passed by her window. Little dust devils danced in the hot afternoon sun while shimmering heat waves made the emaciated, dust-covered people walking listlessly beside the road look more like ghostly apparitions than humans.

The relief workers told her the sad story: The veldt had once been a beautifully green, rolling expanse covered by a newly discovered crop that adapted easily to the climate and soil of that area. Within a few short years, this crop had promised to make the people in the area totally self-sufficient as it became the main, and plentiful, staple of their diet.

Sadly, the relief workers shook their heads as they explained what had happened: The crop had, indeed, become the main staple in the diet of the local people, but too late it had been found to have no nutritional value at all. The tragedy was that hundreds of people had starved to death—with their stomachs full!

Those pitiful African people seem to symbolize many church members in America today who are spiritually starving to death with their stomachs full! We have made the main staples of our "diet" those things that have no real nutritional value—political agendas, social issues, human rights, books about God's Word, musical videos, theological formulas for reaching the postmodern man, and marketing strategies for the local church, along with a myriad of conferences, seminars, retreats, dramas, and "special events." None of these things is harmful in itself, but when substituted for the nutrition of daily Bible reading and prayer, the result is increasing spiritual starvation.

For the past fifteen years as I have crisscrossed America speaking at various conferences, conventions, and churches, I have become convinced of one thing: The average church member is desperately hungry for God's Word. While we read books about it and hear sermons on it and live by principles from it, we are sadly devoid of it on a daily basis. When our lives begin to unravel due to pressure, problems, or pain, we don't seem to know how to access its power and truth in a personal, relevant way that makes a difference. As a result, thousands have spirits that are shriveling even while they are sobbing, "Please, just give me Jesus!"

What does your spiritual diet consist of? Although you may be an active church member and a committed Christian, could it be that you are actually starving for the Bread of Life? Are you starving for the Bread, which is Jesus Himself, offered to you and me through God's Word?

If so, then this journal is for you! It has been designed to take you directly into God's Word. There is no middle man. There are no blanks to fill in. There is not even any cross-referencing required. The simple format for meditation has been developed from my own daily personal time in God's Word as a means of reading a passage in order to hear Him speaking to me personally through it. Day after day, as I use this method in my Bible reading, God has fed me and filled me to overflowing!

As you begin this devotional journal, pray this simple prayer: "Dear God, *please, just give me Jesus!*" Then open your Bible and enjoy the Food!

Anne Graham Lotz

Getting Started

Welcome!

You are about to get started on what for me has been a life-changing journey through John's Gospel. As I have meditated on these Scripture passages describing Jesus' personal interaction with men and women, I have experienced a fresh encounter with Him.

This devotional journal is your map for the journey. Used as a companion to the book *Just Give Me Jesus,* it provides a format for Bible study that is as effective for discussion *groups* (Sunday school classes, women's or men's church groups, home or neighborhood Bible classes, one-on-one discipleship) as it is for an *individual's* private devotions. Believing that God speaks to us individually through His Word, we have designed these worksheets to lead you through a series of questions concerning the designated Scripture passage. The exercises enable you to not only discover for yourself the eternal truths revealed by God in the Bible but also to hear God speaking personally to you through His Word and thus have a fresh encounter with Him.

GETTING STARTED ON YOUR OWN

A DVD of me teaching this simple Bible study format to a Just Give Me Jesus revival audience has been included with this journal to help clarify these techniques.

If you make your way through this journey on your own, using one set of worksheets each day, you will complete the study in a single month. The worksheets have been laid out in thirty "sets" so that, ideally, you can complete one set each day for thirty days. Each set consists of three to five worksheets that will provide a very rich, meaningful pathway for your daily walk with Jesus.

GETTING STARTED IN A GROUP

If you embark on this journey through John's Gospel in a group, you may want to meet once a week to share the insights you've gained. The journal is divided into thirty "daily" portions, which can be used once a week to make up an eight-month-long course of study. Ideally, your group will gather each week under the leadership of a facilitator who will lead you through a meaningful discussion of what you've each discovered individually. If the group is large (twelve or more), you may need to divide into smaller groups for discussion time, with moderators being chosen to lead each one.

The facilitator may offer a summation at the end of the group study, emphasizing specific applications from the Gospel of John to meet the needs and characteristics of your particular group, depending on the age, sex, and interests of the members.

Whether you choose to get started on your own or in a group, I pray that your journey through John's Gospel will result in your own fresh encounter with Jesus!

Tips for a Successful Journey

KNOW WHERE YOU ARE GOING

When I begin a trip, I always look at a map to see where I am going. It helps me know how to get there. A DVD has been included with this journal as your "map" to help you see where you are going and how to get there. It is a live presentation to the Just Give Me Jesus revival audience in Minneapolis, Minnesota the week after 9/11. You can view it straight through, or follow the simple directions on the screen in order to participate in the same way that the audience did.

BE PREPARED

I have taken countless trips in my lifetime—some long, some short, some far, some near. But every single trip involves a certain amount of preparation in order to be successful. And the preparation itself requires a measure of discipline. This journey is no exception.

Spiritual discipline is an essential part of an individual's ability to grow in his or her personal relationship with God through knowledge and understanding of His Word. It is my sincere prayer that whether you use this thirty-day journey through John's gospel in private daily devotions or in a weekly group Bible study, it will provide you with an easy, meaningful format for this growth to occur.

To stay on track and make this study most effective and meaningful to your life, I offer these specific suggestions:

- Set aside a regular *place* for your daily Bible study.

- Set aside a regular *time* for your daily Bible study.

- Pray before beginning each day's journey, asking God to speak to you through His Word.

- Write out your answers for each step of the worksheets in sequence. Do not skip a step.

- Make the time to be still and listen, reflecting thoughtfully on your responses, especially in step 5.

TAKE ONE STEP AT A TIME

STEP 1. LOOK IN GOD'S WORD: Begin by reading the designated passage of Scripture. This is printed for you on each day's devotional section. When you have finished reading the passage, move to step 2.

STEP 2. LIST THE FACTS: Make a verse-by-verse list of the outstanding facts. Don't get caught up in the details; just pinpoint the most obvious facts. Ask yourself who is speaking, what the subject is, where the action is taking place, when it happened, and so on. As you make your list, do not paraphrase but use actual words from the passage itself. Take a moment now to read, on pages 15–18, the completed example of a worksheet focused on Isaiah 55:1–3. When you have read the passage from Isaiah (in step 1), look over the facts listed in step 2 so that you understand these instructions more clearly.

STEP 3. LEARN THE LESSONS: After looking at the passage and listing the facts, you are ready for step 3. Go back to the list of facts in step 2 and look for a lesson to learn from each fact. Ask yourself, *What are the people in this passage doing that I should be doing? Is there a command I should obey? A promise I should claim? A warning I should heed?*

An example I should follow? Look again at the completed example focused on Isaiah 55:1–3. Note (in step 3 of the example) that you may have more than one lesson for each verse.

STEP 4. LISTEN TO HIS VOICE: The fourth step is the most meaningful, but you cannot do it until steps 1, 2, and 3 have been completed. In order to complete step 4, rephrase the lessons you found in 3 and put them in the form of questions you could ask yourself, your spouse, your child, your friend, your neighbor, or your co-worker. As you write out the questions, listen for God to communicate to you personally through His Word.

There are some challenging passages in the Gospel of John. Don't get hung up on what you don't understand. Look for the general principles and lessons that can be learned. An introduction at the beginning of each day's devotion as well as examples offered each day in steps 2, 3, and 4 will help get you started.

Remember, don't rush. It may take you several moments of prayerful meditation to discover meaningful lessons and hear God speaking to you. The object of this devotional journal is not to get through it but to develop your personal relationship with God in order to satisfy your spiritual hunger and increase your spiritual health.

STEP 5. LIVE IT OUT: Read the assigned Scripture passages prayerfully, objectively, thoughtfully, and attentively as you listen for God to speak. He may not speak to you through every verse, but He *will* speak. When He does, record in the step 5 column the verse number, what it is He seems to be saying to you, and your response to Him. You might like to date it as a means not only of keeping a spiritual journal but also of holding yourself accountable to following through in obedience. When you have completed the above five steps, you may want to read the corresponding pages from *Just Give Me Jesus* for further meditation. The page numbers are provided in step 5 at the end of each day's devotion.

God bless you as you seek to learn this simple yet effective method of reading His Word, that you might hear His voice speaking to you personally through it. My prayer is that as you walk daily on this journey through John's Gospel you will learn to love the Bread of Life.

A Completed Worksheet Example:

FOCUSED ON *ISAIAH 55:1–3*

The following worksheet example, focused on Isaiah 55:1–3, has been completed to illustrate the instructions given on pages 12–13. Track each verse carefully through all five steps so you can see how the facts are developed into lessons that then unfold into personal questions and a specific commitment to live in response to what you've learned.

1

LOOK IN GOD'S WORD:

Feel free to underline, circle, or otherwise mark text if it will aid your study.

ISAIAH 55:1 "Come, all you who are thirsty, come to the waters;
and you who have no money,
come, buy and eat!
Come, buy wine and milk
without money and without cost.

²Why spend money on what is not bread, and your labor on what does not satisfy? Listen, listen to me, and eat what is good, and your soul will delight in the richest of fare.

³Give ear and come to me; hear me, that your soul may live. I will make an everlasting covenant with you,
my faithful love promised to David."

2

LIST THE FACTS:

Make a verse-by-verse list of the most outstanding, obvious facts. What does the passage say? Be literal as you answer.

55:1 You who are thirsty, who have no money, come, buy milk without cost.

55:2 Why spend money or labor on what is not bread? Listen, eat what is good.

55:3 Hear me, that your soul may live. I will make a covenant with you.

LEARN THE LESSONS:

What lessons can be learned from these facts? What does the passage mean? Be spiritual as you answer.

55:1 God freely invites us to come to Him through His Word in order to satisfy our spiritual hunger and thirst.

God offers us the spiritual nutrition of His Word as a cost-free soul thirst-quencher.

55:2 Listening to God's voice speak to us personally as we read His Word is worth the time, money, and effort.

"Eating" God's Word by reading, applying, and obeying it is good for us.

55:3 Our spiritual health depends upon our Bible reading.

Through our Bible reading, we enter into a deeper understanding of God's commitment to us and ours to Him.

LISTEN TO HIS VOICE:

What does this passage mean to you? Rewrite the lessons from step 3 in the form of questions. Be personal as you answer.

55:1 How thirsty am I spiritually?

Am I thirsty enough to accept God's invitation to drink the milk of His Word through my active, daily use of this devotional journal?

55:2 What time and effort am I willing to put into this devotional journal?

Will I use this devotional journal as the "utensil" that makes it possible for me to "eat right"?

55:3 Am I physically alive but spiritually starving because I have neglected my Bible reading?

Will I choose to use this devotional journal, not for more head knowledge of God's Word, but to grow in my personal relationship and commitment to God Himself?

5 LIVE IT OUT:

Pinpoint what God is saying to you from this passage. How will you respond? Write down today's date and what you will do now to live it out.

For thirty days, I commit to keeping this journal as a means of satisfying my hunger as I listen for God to speak to me personally through His Word.

Day One

JOHN 1:1–9

Who Is Jesus?

Who is Jesus? How can we know who He really is? We know by studying the truth. One of the few legitimate sources of historical information on His life is found in the four New Testament Gospels, including John's Gospel, which we are studying for the next thirty days.

So who is Jesus? Decide the answer for yourself as you read the apostle John's clear, confident, certain, and compelling biography. His stirring account begins by leaving no doubt that Jesus makes God visible to all, because Jesus is God as Man . . .

LOOK IN GOD'S WORD:

JOHN 1:1 In the beginning was the Word, and the Word was with God, and the Word was God.

²He was with God in the beginning.

³Through him all things were made; without him nothing was made that has been made.

⁴In him was life, and that life was the light of men.

⁵The light shines in the darkness, but the darkness has not understood it.

⁶There came a man who was sent from God; his name was John.

⁷He came as a witness to testify concerning that light, so that through him all men might believe.

⁸He himself was not the light; he came only as a witness to the light.

⁹The true light that gives light to every man was coming into the world.

LIST THE FACTS:

1:1 EXAMPLE: In the beginning the Word that was with God was God.

LEARN THE LESSONS:

3

1:1 EXAMPLE: The mysteries of the beginning of time and space will never be fully explained by science alone.

LISTEN TO HIS VOICE:

4

1:1 EXAMPLE: Do I need to expand my understanding of creation beyond the limits of scientific explanation?

5 **LIVE IT OUT:**

Pinpoint what God is saying to you from this passage. How will you respond? Write down today's date and what you will do now to live it out.

For additional insights on this passage, read *Just Give Me Jesus* pages 1–22.

Day Two

JOHN 1:10–18

I Can See God!

Before Jesus came, God looked down from heaven as man scurried around in panic, unable to cope with the confusion and conflict of life—especially when man's whole world seemed to collapse and life dealt unexpected blows. All man's answers to the problems of pain and evil and death were insufficient. Life just didn't make sense. There seemed to be no order or long-term purpose to it all. And so God became a Man, not just to sort out the confusion and rebuild the collapsed world, but also to offer a new life altogether. Jesus came to make God visible as Man. And that visibility is irresistibly compelling . . .

LOOK IN GOD'S WORD:

JOHN 1:10 He was in the world, and though the world was made through him, the world did not recognize him.

¹¹He came to that which was his own, but his own did not receive him.

¹²Yet to all who received him, to those who believed in his name, he gave the right to become children of God—

¹³children born not of natural descent, nor of human decision or a husband's will, but born of God.

¹⁴The Word became flesh and made his dwelling among us. We have seen his glory, the glory of the One and Only, who came from the Father, full of grace and truth.

¹⁵John testifies concerning him. He cries out, saying, "This was he of whom I said, 'He who comes after me has surpassed me because he was before me.'"

¹⁶From the fullness of his grace we have all received one blessing after another.

¹⁷For the law was given through Moses; grace and truth came through Jesus Christ.

¹⁸No one has ever seen God, but God the One and Only, who is at the Father's side, has made him known.

LIST THE FACTS:

1:10 EXAMPLE: He was in the world, made the world, yet was unrecognized by the world.

LEARN THE LESSONS:

1:10 EXAMPLE: It's possible to be confronted with the person of Jesus Christ yet not recognize Him for Who He is.

LISTEN TO HIS VOICE:

1:10 EXAMPLE: When have I encountered Jesus, and how long did it take me to recognize Him?

5 **LIVE IT OUT:**

Pinpoint what God is saying to you from this passage. How will you respond? Write down today's date and what you will do now to live it out.

For additional insights on this passage, read *Just Give Me Jesus* pages 23–41.

Day Three

JOHN 2:1–11

When the Love Runs Out

Do you feel trapped in a marriage where the love has run out? Have you panicked, looking for escape in an illicit relationship, afternoon fantasies, romance novels, alcohol, or divorce? Or have you resigned yourself to your fate, plunging into a demanding career, the lives of your children, church activities, or community volunteerism in a desperate effort to manage the pain?

Praise God! There is hope. Jesus makes change possible, even when the love runs out.

Marriage is God's idea. If your marriage is broken, take it to Him. The Creator Who made it in the first place can make it work again, which is one reason why God has given you Jesus . . .

Look in God's Word:

John 2:1 On the third day a wedding took place at Cana in Galilee. Jesus' mother was there,

²and Jesus and his disciples had also been invited to the wedding.

³When the wine was gone, Jesus' mother said to him, "They have no more wine."

⁴"Dear woman, why do you involve me?" Jesus replied. "My time has not yet come."

⁵His mother said to the servants, "Do whatever he tells you."

(Continued on page 30.)

List the Facts:

2:1 Example: Jesus, His mother, and His disciples were invited to a wedding in Cana.

3 LEARN THE LESSONS:

2:1 EXAMPLE: Jesus accepts our invitation to come into our marriage.

4 LISTEN TO HIS VOICE:

2:1 EXAMPLE: When have I invited Jesus to come into my marriage?

1

JOHN 2:6 Nearby stood six stone water jars, the kind used by the Jews for ceremonial washing, each holding from twenty to thirty gallons.

[7]Jesus said to the servants, "Fill the jars with water"; so they filled them to the brim.

[8]Then he told them, "Now draw some out and take it to the master of the banquet." They did so,

[9]and the master of the banquet tasted the water that had been turned into wine. He did not realize where it had come from, though the servants who had drawn the water knew. Then he called the bridegroom aside

[10]and said, "Everyone brings out the choice wine first and then the cheaper wine after the guests have had too much to drink; but you have saved the best till now."

[11]This, the first of his miraculous signs, Jesus performed at Cana in Galilee. He thus revealed his glory, and his disciples put their faith in him.

2

3 LEARN THE LESSONS:

4 LISTEN TO HIS VOICE:

5 LIVE IT OUT:

Pinpoint what God is saying to you from this passage. How will you respond? Write down today's date and what you will do now to live it out.

For additional insights from this passage, read *Just Give Me Jesus* pages 44–62.

Day Four

JOHN 3:1–8

The Basic Necessity

Is something missing in your life, something you can't define? Perhaps all you know is that life doesn't seem to be enough for you.

Has your search for joy, happiness, and meaning caused you to climb upward in your career, seek a higher position, devote yourself to greater success in your business? When that didn't work, did you decide you needed a way of drawing attention to yourself by increasing your public reputation, visibility, or fame? Did you become more frustrated when that turned out to be another dead end? Perhaps then you rushed to find a way of remaking your image through cosmetic surgery, dieting, weightlifting, jogging, an exercise video, or a membership at the spa where you sculpted your body? As a last act of desperation, did you throw yourself into pleasurable pursuits, entertainment, fun? As a result, do you find that at this moment you are beyond frustration and totally exhausted in soul and spirit? You've just died on the inside. Hasn't anyone told you? You need the basic Necessity for real life. You need Jesus. He makes change possible when life isn't enough . . .

LOOK IN GOD'S WORD:

JOHN 3:1 Now there was a man of the Pharisees named Nicodemus, a member of the Jewish ruling council.

²He came to Jesus at night and said, "Rabbi, we know you are a teacher who has come from God. For no one could perform the miraculous signs you are doing if God were not with him."

³In reply Jesus declared, "I tell you the truth, no one can see the kingdom of God unless he is born again."

⁴"How can a man be born when he is old?" Nicodemus asked. "Surely he cannot enter a second time into his mother's womb to be born!"

⁵Jesus answered, "I tell you the truth, no one can enter the kingdom of God unless he is born of water and the Spirit.

⁶Flesh gives birth to flesh, but the Spirit gives birth to spirit.

⁷You should not be surprised at my saying, 'You must be born again.'

⁸The wind blows wherever it pleases. You hear its sound, but you cannot tell where it comes from or where it is going. So it is with everyone born of the Spirit."

LIST THE FACTS:

3:1 EXAMPLE: Nicodemus was a Pharisee and a member of the ruling council.

LEARN THE LESSONS:

3:1 EXAMPLE: God not only knows us by name, but also knows the extent of our devotion to Him.

LISTEN TO HIS VOICE:

3:1 EXAMPLE: Would God describe my devotion to Him as traditional religion or a personal relationship?

5 LIVE IT OUT:

Pinpoint what God is saying to you from this passage. How will you respond?
Write down today's date and what you will do now to live it out.

For additional insights on this passage, read *Just Give Me Jesus* pages 63–75.

Day Five

How Can I Start Over?

Jesus sought to explain in simple, relevant terms the answer to Nicodemus's question, "How can a man be born when he is old?" But Nicodemus began to resist the truth. He interrupted Jesus' explanation by blurting out incredulously, "How can this be?"

Thousands of men and women throughout the ages have experienced the life-changing impact of the words Nicodemus had the privilege of hearing first. But those generations of believers have also had the advantage of New Testament teaching. It's hard to imagine how stunning Jesus' words must have been to a man who heard them with an Old Testament perspective. It's understandable that Nicodemus was unable to quickly grasp such a profound yet basic concept. Even now, two thousand years later, we marvel at the beautiful way God has provided what we need most. Being born again is God's solution to our need for love and life and light. Regardless of your age, you can start over . . .

1 LOOK IN GOD'S WORD:

JOHN 3:9 "How can this be?" Nicodemus asked.

¹⁰"You are Israel's teacher," said Jesus, "and do you not understand these things?

¹¹I tell you the truth, we speak of what we know, and we testify to what we have seen, but still you people do not accept our testimony.

¹²I have spoken to you of earthly things and you do not believe; how then will you believe if I speak of heavenly things?

¹³No one has ever gone into heaven except the one who came from heaven—the Son of Man.

¹⁴Just as Moses lifted up the snake in the desert, so the Son of Man must be lifted up,

¹⁵that everyone who believes in him may have eternal life."

(Continued on page 40.)

2 LIST THE FACTS:

3:9 EXAMPLE: Nicodemus asked how.

LEARN THE LESSONS:

3:9 EXAMPLE: When we don't understand what God has said, we can ask Him for further insight.

LISTEN TO HIS VOICE:

3:9 EXAMPLE: What questions have I had during this study that I need to bring to Jesus?

LOOK IN GOD'S WORD:

1

JOHN 3:16 "For God so loved the world that he gave his one and only Son, that whoever believes in him shall not perish but have eternal life.

¹⁷For God did not send his Son into the world to condemn the world, but to save the world through him.

¹⁸Whoever believes in him is not condemned, but whoever does not believe stands condemned already because he has not believed in the name of God's one and only Son.

¹⁹This is the verdict: Light has come into the world, but men loved darkness instead of light because their deeds were evil.

²⁰Everyone who does evil hates the light, and will not come into the light for fear that his deeds will be exposed.

²¹But whoever lives by the truth comes into the light, so that it may be seen plainly that what he has done has been done through God."

LIST THE FACTS:

2

3 **LEARN THE LESSONS:**

4 **LISTEN TO HIS VOICE:**

LIVE IT OUT:

5 Pinpoint what God is saying to you from this passage. How will you respond? Write down today's date and what you will do now to live it out.

For additional insights on this passage, read *Just Give Me Jesus* pages 75–89.

Day Six

JOHN 4:1–10

A Divine Appointment

After visiting with Nicodemus, Jesus headed into the Judean countryside with His small band of disciples. As people began flocking to Him, rumors about His popularity and ministry began to develop into a controversy that threatened to divide His followers from those of His cousin and forerunner, John the Baptist. Rather than lend fuel to the fires of gossip and jealousy, Jesus quietly withdrew, returning to Galilee. On His journey through Samaria He had a divine appointment with one woman—an outcast from society—who was running on empty . . .

LOOK IN GOD'S WORD:

JOHN 4:1 The Pharisees heard that Jesus was gaining and baptizing more disciples than John,

²although in fact it was not Jesus who baptized, but his disciples.

³When the Lord learned of this, he left Judea and went back once more to Galilee.

⁴Now he had to go through Samaria.

⁵So he came to a town in Samaria called Sychar, near the plot of ground Jacob had given to his son Joseph.

⁶Jacob's well was there, and Jesus, tired as he was from the journey, sat down by the well. It was about the sixth hour.

⁷When a Samaritan woman came to draw water, Jesus said to her, "Will you give me a drink?"

⁸(His disciples had gone into the town to buy food.)

⁹The Samaritan woman said to him, "You are a Jew and I am a Samaritan woman. How can you ask me for a drink?" (For Jews do not associate with Samaritans.)

¹⁰Jesus answered her, "If you knew the gift of God and who it is that asks you for a drink, you would have asked him and he would have given you living water."

LIST THE FACTS:

4:1 EXAMPLE: The Pharisees heard that Jesus baptized more disciples than John.

LEARN THE LESSONS:

4:1 EXAMPLE: We need to beware of hearsay within the church.

LISTEN TO HIS VOICE:

4:1 EXAMPLE: On what am I basing my opinions—on hearsay or on the truth?

5 LIVE IT OUT:

Pinpoint what God is saying to you from this passage. How will you respond? Write down today's date and what you will do now to live it out.

For additional insights on this passage, read *Just Give Me Jesus* pages 91–102.

Day Seven

JOHN 4:11–26

I'm Thirsty!

The Samaritan woman was drawn to Jesus, perhaps in spite of herself, and desperately began to want more in life. Her emptiness and unhappiness became suddenly, overwhelmingly unbearable. So in the only way she knew, she humbly asked for the Living Water. Even though she was confused, she reached out to take what He offered.

As He listened not only to the words the woman spoke but also to the thoughts in her mind and the emotions of her heart, He must have been deeply moved, which was why this passage tells us "he had to go through Samaria." At this point, you would think He would give her the Living Water. After all, that was what He wanted to do. And she was so close. But one thing still stood in the way of her receiving it . . .

LOOK IN GOD'S WORD:

JOHN 4:11 "Sir," the woman said, "you have nothing to draw with and the well is deep. Where can you get this living water?

¹²Are you greater than our father Jacob, who gave us the well and drank from it himself, as did also his sons and his flocks and herds?"

¹³Jesus answered, "Everyone who drinks this water will be thirsty again,

¹⁴but whoever drinks the water I give him will never thirst. Indeed, the water I give him will become in him a spring of water welling up to eternal life."

¹⁵The woman said to him, "Sir, give me this water so that I won't get thirsty and have to keep coming here to draw water."

¹⁶He told her, "Go, call your husband and come back."

¹⁷"I have no husband," she replied. Jesus said to her, "You are right when you say you have no husband.

¹⁸The fact is, you have had five husbands, and the man you now have is not your husband. What you have just said is quite true."

(Continued on page 50.)

LIST THE FACTS:

4:11 EXAMPLE: The woman said, "You have nothing to draw with. Where can you get water?"

LEARN THE LESSONS:

4:11 EXAMPLE: Sometimes we don't understand that Jesus wants to give us spiritual blessings, not material ones.

LISTEN TO HIS VOICE:

4:11 EXAMPLE: What blessing from God am I missing because I'm focused on material things?

1 LOOK IN GOD'S WORD:

JOHN 4:19 "Sir," the woman said, "I can see that you are a prophet.

20Our fathers worshiped on this mountain, but you Jews claim that the place where we must worship is in Jerusalem."

21Jesus declared, "Believe me, woman, a time is coming when you will worship the Father neither on this mountain nor in Jerusalem.

22You Samaritans worship what you do not know; we worship what we do know, for salvation is from the Jews.

23Yet a time is coming and has now come when the true worshipers will worship the Father in spirit and truth, for they are the kind of worshipers the Father seeks.

24God is spirit, and his worshipers must worship in spirit and in truth."

25The woman said, "I know that Messiah" (called Christ) "is coming. When he comes, he will explain everything to us."

26Then Jesus declared, "I who speak to you am he."

2 LIST THE FACTS:

3 LEARN THE LESSONS:

4 LISTEN TO HIS VOICE:

5 **LIVE IT OUT:**

Pinpoint what God is saying to you from this passage. How will you respond? Write down today's date and what you will do now to live it out.

For additional insights on this passage, read *Just Give Me Jesus* pages 102–111.

Day Eight

JOHN 4:27–42

I Found It!

I find myself from time to time running on empty.

In the busyness of ministry,

the pressures of responsibility,

the demands of family,

the weariness of activity,

the excitement of opportunity,

I sometimes wake up and realize, *I am so dry and thirsty*. Invariably, when I examine myself, the reason for the dryness of spirit can be traced to one thing: I'm not drinking freely of the Water of Life. I'm neglecting my Bible study. I'm rushing through my prayer time. I'm not listening to the voice of the Lord because I'm just too busy to be still. At those times I carve out quiet interludes to confess my sins and read and meditate and pray and listen and just drink Him in.

Thank You, dear God, for still giving Living Water from the Well that never goes dry . . .

Look in God's Word:

John 4:27 Just then his disciples returned and were surprised to find him talking with a woman. But no one asked, "What do you want?" or "Why are you talking with her?"

28Then, leaving her water jar, the woman went back to the town and said to the people,

29"Come, see a man who told me everything I ever did. Could this be the Christ?"

30They came out of the town and made their way toward him.

31Meanwhile his disciples urged him, "Rabbi, eat something."

32But he said to them, "I have food to eat that you know nothing about."

33Then his disciples said to each other, "Could someone have brought him food?"

34"My food," said Jesus, "is to do the will of him who sent me and to finish his work."

(Continued on page 56.)

List the Facts:

4:27 Example: The disciples were surprised to find Jesus talking with a woman, but no one asked why.

LEARN THE LESSONS:

4:27 EXAMPLE: Some Christians find it surprising when God singles out women and minorities for special attention.

LISTEN TO HIS VOICE:

4:27 EXAMPLE: What cultural prejudices do I have that are challenged by Jesus' own example?

LOOK IN GOD'S WORD:

JOHN 4:35 "Do you not say, 'Four months more and then the harvest'? I tell you, open your eyes and look at the fields! They are ripe for harvest.

[36]Even now the reaper draws his wages, even now he harvests the crop for eternal life, so that the sower and the reaper may be glad together.

[37]Thus the saying 'One sows and another reaps' is true.

[38]I sent you to reap what you have not worked for. Others have done the hard work, and you have reaped the benefits of their labor."

[39]Many of the Samaritans from that town believed in him because of the woman's testimony, "He told me everything I ever did."

[40]So when the Samaritans came to him, they urged him to stay with them, and he stayed two days.

[41]And because of his words many more became believers.

[42]They said to the woman, "We no longer believe just because of what you said; now we have heard for ourselves, and we know that this man really is the Savior of the world."

LIST THE FACTS:

3 **LEARN THE LESSONS:**

4 **LISTEN TO HIS VOICE:**

5 Live It Out:

Pinpoint what God is saying to you from this passage. How will you respond? Write down today's date and what you will do now to live it out.

For additional insights on this passage, read *Just Give Me Jesus* pages 111–113.

Day Nine

JOHN 5:1-9

Waiting for the Angel

The pool by the Sheep Gate in Jerusalem was very probably circular but enclosed by five breezeways that formed a pentagon, with each of its five sides made up of a porch covered by an arch. Possibly it was a mineral or sulfur spring that bubbled out of the ground, drawing the attention of the desperately hopeless who believed it to possess healing, curative powers. It was around this pool, under the covered arches, that those who were bypassed by the rest of society gathered, focusing on the legend that said when an angel caused the water to bubble up, the first person into it would be healed . . .

LOOK IN GOD'S WORD:

JOHN 5:1 Some time later, Jesus went up to Jerusalem for a feast of the Jews.

²Now there is in Jerusalem near the Sheep Gate a pool, which in Aramaic is called Bethesda and which is surrounded by five covered colonnades.

³Here a great number of disabled people used to lie—the blind, the lame, the paralyzed.*

⁵One who was there had been an invalid for thirty-eight years.

⁶When Jesus saw him lying there and learned that he had been in this condition for a long time, he asked him, "Do you want to get well?"

⁷"Sir," the invalid replied, "I have no one to help me into the pool when the water is stirred. While I am trying to get in, someone else goes down ahead of me."

⁸Then Jesus said to him, "Get up! Pick up your mat and walk."

⁹At once the man was cured; he picked up his mat and walked. The day on which this took place was a Sabbath.

LIST THE FACTS:

5:1 EXAMPLE: Jesus went to Jerusalem for a feast.

* Some manuscripts include the phrase "paralyzed—and they waited for the moving of the waters." Verse 4 does not appear in the better manuscripts and has been omitted here.

LEARN THE LESSONS:

3 **5:1 EXAMPLE:** We need to make an effort to be involved in the life of the church.

LISTEN TO HIS VOICE:

4 **5:1 EXAMPLE:** What effort am I making to be involved in my church?

5 LIVE IT OUT:

Pinpoint what God is saying to you from this passage. How will you respond? Write down today's date and what you will do now to live it out.

For additional insights on this passage, read *Just Give Me Jesus* pages 114–128.

Day Ten

JOHN 6:1–14

Jesus Knows My Needs

Jesus saw the physical, emotional, and spiritual needs of His friends and knew the solution was a time of quiet rest and reflection. And He knows the solution is the same for you and me today. So He invites us, as He did His disciples, "Come with Me by yourself to a quiet place and get some rest."

It was Passover time, it was a national holiday, it was springtime, and it must have seemed the perfect day to join Jesus for a picnic in the hills.

I wonder how the disciples felt as they looked up and saw the trickle of people coming around the end of the lake. I wonder how they felt when they saw the trickle grow into a river that grew into a flood of five thousand men, not counting women and children. Jesus gave up His time to Himself, He gave up His "holiday," He gave up His "family" time in order to meet the needs of the crowd. He knew that meeting the needs of others invariably requires some personal sacrifice . . .

LOOK IN GOD'S WORD:

JOHN 6:1 Some time after this, Jesus crossed to the far shore of the Sea of Galilee (that is, the Sea of Tiberias),

²and a great crowd of people followed him because they saw the miraculous signs he had performed on the sick.

³Then Jesus went up on a mountainside and sat down with his disciples.

⁴The Jewish Passover Feast was near.

⁵When Jesus looked up and saw a great crowd coming toward him, he said to Philip, "Where shall we buy bread for these people to eat?"

⁶He asked this only to test him, for he already had in mind what he was going to do.

⁷Philip answered him, "Eight months' wages would not buy enough bread for each one to have a bite!"

(Continued on page 66.)

LIST THE FACTS:

6:1 EXAMPLE: Jesus crossed Galilee.

LEARN THE LESSONS:

3

6:1 EXAMPLE: It's not always God's will for us to stay in one place.

LISTEN TO HIS VOICE:

4

6:1 EXAMPLE: Is it time for me to move on in my Christian experience?

JOHN 6:8 Another of his disciples, Andrew, Simon Peter's brother, spoke up,

⁹"Here is a boy with five small barley loaves and two small fish, but how far will they go among so many?"

¹⁰Jesus said, "Have the people sit down." There was plenty of grass in that place, and the men sat down, about five thousand of them.

¹¹Jesus then took the loaves, gave thanks, and distributed to those who were seated as much as they wanted. He did the same with the fish.

¹²When they had all had enough to eat, he said to his disciples, "Gather the pieces that are left over. Let nothing be wasted."

¹³So they gathered them and filled twelve baskets with the pieces of the five barley loaves left over by those who had eaten.

¹⁴After the people saw the miraculous sign that Jesus did, they began to say, "Surely this is the Prophet who is to come into the world."

3 LEARN THE LESSONS:

4 LISTEN TO HIS VOICE:

LIVE IT OUT:

Pinpoint what God is saying to you from this passage. How will you respond? Write down today's date and what you will do now to live it out.

For additional insights on this passage, read *Just Give Me Jesus* pages 130–151.

Day Eleven

JOHN 14:15–26

Jesus in Me

A lot of Christians I know are trying to live the Christian life without ever activating the power. It may be possible to get some things done without power, but the effort and the struggle will make most want to quit. And the power is not so much a "what" as a "Who." The power is the person of the Holy Spirit.

There are times when I have gotten the distinct impression from some Christians that the Holy Spirit is an optional extra, reserved primarily for benedictions, baptisms, and those we label "charismatics." Others give the impression that He is more like a heavenly genie in a bottle, Who, if you rub Him with the right mixture of prayer and faith, will perform miracles for you. But the Holy Spirit is not an optional extra! He is not to be reserved only for special occasions or exclusive groups, nor is He a trick-performing genie. He is a divine necessity Who is imparted to each and every believer at the moment of conversion. He is Jesus in me . . .

LOOK IN GOD'S WORD:

JOHN 14:15 "If you love me, you will obey what I command.

¹⁶And I will ask the Father, and he will give you another Counselor to be with you forever—

¹⁷the Spirit of truth. The world cannot accept him, because it neither sees him nor knows him. But you know him, for he lives with you and will be in you.

¹⁸I will not leave you as orphans; I will come to you.

¹⁹Before long, the world will not see me anymore, but you will see me. Because I live, you also will live.

²⁰On that day you will realize that I am in my Father, and you are in me, and I am in you.

²¹Whoever has my commands and obeys them, he is the one who loves me. He who loves me will be loved by my Father, and I too will love him and show myself to him."

(Continued on page 72.)

LIST THE FACTS:

14:15 EXAMPLE: If you love Me, you will obey.

LEARN THE LESSONS:

14:15 EXAMPLE: Obedience to God's Word is proof of our love for Jesus.

LISTEN TO HIS VOICE:

14:15 EXAMPLE: If I say I love Jesus, what proof can others find in my life?

LOOK IN GOD'S WORD:

2

LIST THE FACTS:

JOHN 14:22 Then Judas (not Judas Iscariot) said, "But, Lord, why do you intend to show yourself to us and not to the world?"

²³Jesus replied, "If anyone loves me, he will obey my teaching. My Father will love him, and we will come to him and make our home with him.

²⁴He who does not love me will not obey my teaching. These words you hear are not my own; they belong to the Father who sent me.

²⁵"All this I have spoken while still with you.

²⁶But the Counselor, the Holy Spirit, whom the Father will send in my name, will teach you all things and will remind you of everything I have said to you."

3 **LEARN THE LESSONS:**

4 **LISTEN TO HIS VOICE:**

LIVE IT OUT:

Pinpoint what God is saying to you from this passage. How will you respond? Write down today's date and what you will do now to live it out.

For additional insights on this passage, read *Just Give Me Jesus* pages 152–172.

Day Twelve

JOHN 9:1–12

The Problem of Pain

The problem of pain and questions about suffering are as old as the human race. But they remain the clinical subject of philosophical theories and intellectual sparring and theological debate until they become personal, until it's *our* homes or *our* children or *our* loved ones who are hurting. Then we simply have desperate questions that need direct answers.

The disciples had been so sure that suffering was a punishment for someone's fault that it was a totally new thought to consider suffering as a powerful and personal opportunity to glorify God . . .

Look in God's Word:

John 9:1 As he went along, he saw a man blind from birth.

²His disciples asked him, "Rabbi, who sinned, this man or his parents, that he was born blind?"

³"Neither this man nor his parents sinned," said Jesus, "but this happened so that the work of God might be displayed in his life.

⁴As long as it is day, we must do the work of him who sent me. Night is coming, when no one can work.

⁵While I am in the world, I am the light of the world."

⁶Having said this, he spit on the ground, made some mud with the saliva, and put it on the man's eyes.

⁷"Go," he told him, "wash in the Pool of Siloam" (this word means Sent). So the man went and washed, and came home seeing.

(Continued on page 78.)

List the Facts:

9:1 Example: As Jesus went, He saw a blind man.

LEARN THE LESSONS:

3

9:1 EXAMPLE: In the midst of our busyness, we need to pay attention to the needs of those around us.

LISTEN TO HIS VOICE:

4

9:1 EXAMPLE: Whose need am I ignoring because I am so preoccupied with my own interests and concerns?

1. LOOK IN GOD'S WORD:

JOHN 9:8 His neighbors and those who had formerly seen him begging asked, "Isn't this the same man who used to sit and beg?"

⁹Some claimed that he was. Others said, "No, he only looks like him." But he himself insisted, "I am the man."

¹⁰"How then were your eyes opened?" they demanded.

¹¹He replied, "The man they call Jesus made some mud and put it on my eyes. He told me to go to Siloam and wash. So I went and washed, and then I could see."

¹²"Where is this man?" they asked him. "I don't know," he said.

2. LIST THE FACTS:

3 **LEARN THE LESSONS:**

4 **LISTEN TO HIS VOICE:**

5 LIVE IT OUT:

Pinpoint what God is saying to you from this passage. How will you respond? Write down today's date and what you will do now to live it out.

For additional insights on this passage, read *Just Give Me Jesus* pages 174–190.

Day Thirteen

JOHN 9:13–23

More Than a Man

After having heard the former blind man's personal witness, his friends and neighbors apparently felt that the authorities should be informed before this kind of thing got out of hand. So the man was dragged before the religious leaders. Under the sharp, critical questioning of the Pharisees, rather than being intimidated, the man's thoughts were stimulated. He used the interrogation as an opportunity to publicly tell others what had happened in his life. As he answered questions, his faith developed rapidly and he came to the conclusion that the One he had thought was just a man was actually a prophet . . .

LOOK IN GOD'S WORD:

JOHN 9:13 They brought to the Pharisees the man who had been blind.

¹⁴Now the day on which Jesus had made the mud and opened the man's eyes was a Sabbath.

¹⁵Therefore the Pharisees also asked him how he had received his sight. "He put mud on my eyes," the man replied, "and I washed, and now I see."

¹⁶Some of the Pharisees said, "This man is not from God, for he does not keep the Sabbath." But others asked, "How can a sinner do such miraculous signs?" So they were divided.

¹⁷Finally they turned again to the blind man, "What have you to say about him? It was your eyes he opened." The man replied, "He is a prophet."

(Continued on page 84.)

LIST THE FACTS:

9:13 EXAMPLE: They brought the former blind man to the Pharisees.

LEARN THE LESSONS:

9:13 EXAMPLE: The world is still trying to figure out the difference Jesus makes in people's lives.

LISTEN TO HIS VOICE:

9:13 EXAMPLE: Who is seeking an explanation for the difference Jesus has made in my life?

1. LOOK IN GOD'S WORD:

JOHN 9:18 The Jews still did not believe that he had been blind and had received his sight until they sent for the man's parents.

[19]"Is this your son?" they asked. "Is this the one you say was born blind? How is it that now he can see?"

[20]"We know he is our son," the parents answered, "and we know he was born blind.

[21]But how he can see now, or who opened his eyes, we don't know. Ask him. He is of age; he will speak for himself."

[22]His parents said this because they were afraid of the Jews, for already the Jews had decided that anyone who acknowledged that Jesus was the Christ would be put out of the synagogue.

[23]That was why his parents said, "He is of age; ask him."

2. LIST THE FACTS:

3 **LEARN THE LESSONS:**

4 **LISTEN TO HIS VOICE:**

5 LIVE IT OUT:

Pinpoint what God is saying to you from this passage. How will you respond? Write down today's date and what you will do now to live it out.

For additional insights on this passage, read *Just Give Me Jesus* pages 190–191.

Day Fourteen

JOHN 9:24–34

One Thing I Know

The former blind man could not debate these religious authorities on their level. He did not have all the theological, intellectual, philosophical answers to their questions. But he did have his own experience that no one could take away from him. With what must have been a head held high and eyes that were probably still stinging and watering from the unaccustomed light, he looked straight back at his accusers and declared with simplicity and humility, "One thing I do know. I was blind but now I see!" . . .

JOHN 9:24 A second time they summoned the man who had been blind. "Give glory to God," they said. "We know this man is a sinner."

²⁵He replied, "Whether he is a sinner or not, I don't know. One thing I do know. I was blind but now I see!"

²⁶Then they asked him, "What did he do to you? How did he open your eyes?"

²⁷He answered, "I have told you already and you did not listen. Why do you want to hear it again? Do you want to become his disciples, too?"

²⁸Then they hurled insults at him and said, "You are this fellow's disciple! We are disciples of Moses!

(Continued on page 90.)

9:24 EXAMPLE: The former blind man was interrogated a second time by the Pharisees.

LEARN THE LESSONS:

3

9:24 EXAMPLE: Sometimes organized religion is the true believer's bitterest skeptic.

LISTEN TO HIS VOICE:

4

9:24 EXAMPLE: Who has voiced skepticism of the difference Jesus has made in my life?

LOOK IN GOD'S WORD:

JOHN 9:29 We know that God spoke to Moses, but as for this fellow, we don't even know where he comes from."

30The man answered, "Now that is remarkable! You don't know where he comes from, yet he opened my eyes.

31We know that God does not listen to sinners. He listens to the godly man who does his will.

32Nobody has ever heard of opening the eyes of a man born blind.

33If this man were not from God, he could do nothing."

34To this they replied, "You were steeped in sin at birth; how dare you lecture us!" And they threw him out.

LIST THE FACTS:

3 LEARN THE LESSONS:

4 LISTEN TO HIS VOICE:

5 LIVE IT OUT:

Pinpoint what God is saying to you from this passage. How will you respond? Write down today's date and what you will do now to live it out.

For additional insights on this passage, read *Just Give Me Jesus* pages 191–192.

Day Fifteen

JOHN 9:35–41

Upside Down and Inside Out

The Pharisees threw the man out of the temple. He was publicly disgraced by the religious leaders of his day and because of the excommunication, he would be considered a moral leper in Jerusalem with no social respectability. How did he feel? Looking back on his day, it must have seemed like a dream that had turned into a nightmare! How could something so fantastically good become something so horribly bad?

In one day, the former blind man's life had turned upside down and inside out. As he must have wandered in a daze through the narrow, crowded streets, surely he tried to comprehend all he had experienced, realizing that although he had gained his physical sight he had lost any social acceptance he would ever hope to have . . .

LOOK IN GOD'S WORD:

JOHN 9:35 Jesus heard that they had thrown him out, and when he found him, he said, "Do you believe in the Son of Man?"

[36]"Who is he, sir?" the man asked. "Tell me so that I may believe in him."

[37]Jesus said, "You have now seen him; in fact, he is the one speaking with you."

[38]Then the man said, "Lord, I believe," and he worshiped him.

[39]Jesus said, "For judgment I have come into this world, so that the blind will see and those who see will become blind."

[40]Some Pharisees who were with him heard him say this and asked, "What? Are we blind too?"

[41]Jesus said, "If you were blind, you would not be guilty of sin; but now that you claim you can see, your guilt remains."

LIST THE FACTS:

9:35 EXAMPLE: Jesus heard the man had been thrown out, found him, and asked if he believed.

3 LEARN THE LESSONS:

9:35 EXAMPLE: Jesus knows about our persecution, draws near to us, and uses it to strengthen our faith.

4 LISTEN TO HIS VOICE:

9:35 EXAMPLE: Why do I feel isolated and alone when criticized for my relationship with Jesus?

5 LIVE IT OUT:

Pinpoint what God is saying to you from this passage. How will you respond? Write down today's date and what you will do now to live it out.

For additional insights on this passage, read *Just Give Me Jesus* pages 192–197.

Day Sixteen

JOHN 11:1–6

When God Is Silent

Do you have a prayer that has remained unanswered? Does God seem to be hiding Himself from you? *Why does He delay?* Why does He allow you and your loved ones to suffer so? One reason for His delay seems to be to allow us time to exhaust every other avenue of help until we come to the conclusion, without any doubt, that we are totally helpless without Him, and we rest our faith in Him and Him alone.

Jesus' delay in answering our prayers is never due to indifference or preoccupation with other things or an inability to act. His delay has a purpose . . .

LOOK IN GOD'S WORD:

JOHN 11:1 Now a man named Lazarus was sick. He was from Bethany, the village of Mary and her sister Martha.

²This Mary, whose brother Lazarus now lay sick, was the same one who poured perfume on the Lord and wiped his feet with her hair.

³So the sisters sent word to Jesus, "Lord, the one you love is sick."

⁴When he heard this, Jesus said, "This sickness will not end in death. No, it is for God's glory so that God's Son may be glorified through it."

⁵Jesus loved Martha and her sister and Lazarus.

⁶Yet when he heard that Lazarus was sick, he stayed where he was two more days.

LIST THE FACTS:

11:1 EXAMPLE: Lazarus, from Bethany, the village of Mary and Martha, was sick.

LEARN THE LESSONS:

11:1 EXAMPLE: Bad things happen to some people and not to others.

LISTEN TO HIS VOICE:

11:1 EXAMPLE: What bad thing has happened to someone I love?

5 Live It Out:

Pinpoint what God is saying to you from this passage. How will you respond? Write down today's date and what you will do now to live it out.

For additional insights on this passage, read *Just Give Me Jesus* pages 198–204.

Day Seventeen

JOHN 11:7–16

The Confusing and Perfect Ways of God

God's delays and His ways can be confusing because the process God uses to accomplish His will can go against human logic and common sense. The reason for this is to focus our faith, not in our friends or our abilities or resources or knowledge or strength or anything other than Him alone.

Jesus knew Mary and Martha's prayer would be answered, but in a totally different way than they had asked. And Jesus knew much better than His disciples what awaited Him this time in Jerusalem, yet it was for this very time that He had been born . . .

Look in God's Word:

John 11:7 Then he said to his disciples, "Let us go back to Judea."

8"But Rabbi," they said, "a short while ago the Jews tried to stone you, and yet you are going back there?"

9Jesus answered, "Are there not twelve hours of daylight? A man who walks by day will not stumble, for he sees by this world's light.

10It is when he walks by night that he stumbles, for he has no light."

11After he had said this, he went on to tell them, "Our friend Lazarus has fallen asleep; but I am going there to wake him up."

12His disciples replied, "Lord, if he sleeps, he will get better."

13Jesus had been speaking of his death, but his disciples thought he meant natural sleep.

14So then he told them plainly, "Lazarus is dead,

15and for your sake I am glad I was not there, so that you may believe. But let us go to him."

16Then Thomas (called Didymus) said to the rest of the disciples, "Let us also go, that we may die with him."

List the Facts:

11:7 Example: Jesus said, "Let's go back."

3 LEARN THE LESSONS:

11:7 EXAMPLE: God's Word reveals His intentions.

4 LISTEN TO HIS VOICE:

11:7 EXAMPLE: How can I know what God is intending to do if I'm not reading His Word?

5 LIVE IT OUT:

Pinpoint what God is saying to you from this passage. How will you respond? Write down today's date and what you will do now to live it out.

For additional insights on this passage, read *Just Give Me Jesus* pages 204–209.

Day Eighteen

JOHN 11:17–27

Do You Believe?

Jesus patiently persisted in developing Martha's faith until it was focused on Him, and Him alone. With eyes that must have seemed to penetrate past her doubting mind and into her bleeding heart to the very depths of her being, He replied with words that have resonated through the centuries, giving hope at the gravesides of thousands of believers of every generation, "I am the resurrection and the life. He who believes in me will live, even though he dies; and whoever lives and believes in me will never die. Do you believe this?" (John 11:25–26). *Do you believe this . . . ?*

1

LOOK IN GOD'S WORD:

JOHN 11:17 On his arrival, Jesus found that Lazarus had already been in the tomb for four days.

18Bethany was less than two miles from Jerusalem,

19and many Jews had come to Martha and Mary to comfort them in the loss of their brother.

20When Martha heard that Jesus was coming, she went out to meet him, but Mary stayed at home.

21"Lord," Martha said to Jesus, "if you had been here, my brother would not have died.

22But I know that even now God will give you whatever you ask."

23Jesus said to her, "Your brother will rise again."

24Martha answered, "I know he will rise again in the resurrection at the last day."

25Jesus said to her, "I am the resurrection and the life. He who believes in me will live, even though he dies;

26and whoever lives and believes in me will never die. Do you believe this?"

27"Yes, Lord," she told him, "I believe that you are the Christ, the Son of God, who was to come into the world."

LIST THE FACTS:

11:17 EXAMPLE: On his arrival, Jesus found Lazarus had been entombed four days.

3 LEARN THE LESSONS:

11:17 EXAMPLE: Some situations seem so final they are hopeless.

4 LISTEN TO HIS VOICE:

11:17 EXAMPLE: Who do I know who's been spiritually dead in sin so long that I think he or she is beyond hope?

5 LIVE IT OUT:

Pinpoint what God is saying to you from this passage. How will you respond? Write down today's date and what you will do now to live it out.

For additional insights on this passage, read *Just Give Me Jesus* pages 210–213.

Day Nineteen

JOHN 11:28–37

The Sparkling Jewel of Hope

Just as a diamond seems to sparkle more brilliantly when displayed in a black velvet case, so the radiant beauty of Christlike character seems to shine more splendidly against the backdrop of suffering. Even in Martha's grief, the jewel of hope that seemed to have been birthed in her spirit sparkled . . .

LOOK IN GOD'S WORD:

1

JOHN 11:28 And after she had said this, she went back and called her sister Mary aside. "The Teacher is here," she said, "and is asking for you."

²⁹When Mary heard this, she got up quickly and went to him.

³⁰Now Jesus had not yet entered the village, but was still at the place where Martha had met him.

³¹When the Jews who had been with Mary in the house, comforting her, noticed how quickly she got up and went out, they followed her, supposing she was going to the tomb to mourn there.

³²When Mary reached the place where Jesus was and saw him, she fell at his feet and said, "Lord, if you had been here, my brother would not have died."

³³When Jesus saw her weeping, and the Jews who had come along with her also weeping, he was deeply moved in spirit and troubled.

³⁴"Where have you laid him?" he asked. "Come and see, Lord," they replied.

³⁵Jesus wept.

³⁶Then the Jews said, "See how he loved him!"

³⁷But some of them said, "Could not he who opened the eyes of the blind man have kept this man from dying?"

LIST THE FACTS:

2

11:28 EXAMPLE: Martha called Mary and said, "The Teacher is here and is asking for you."

3 LEARN THE LESSONS:

11:28 EXAMPLE: We need to tell our "sister" about Jesus.

4 LISTEN TO HIS VOICE:

11:28 EXAMPLE: What "sister" do I need to tell about Jesus?

5 LIVE IT OUT:

Pinpoint what God is saying to you from this passage. How will you respond? Write down today's date and what you will do now to live it out.

For additional insights on this passage, read *Just Give Me Jesus* pages 213–218.

Day Twenty

JOHN 11:38–44

Faith That Works

Just as the blind man had to obey the command of Jesus and wash his eyes before he could see, just as the paralyzed man had to get up and take up his bed and walk before he found the power he had been given to do so, just as the man with the shriveled hand had to stretch it forth before it was made whole, so you and I have to demonstrate our faith in God's Word through our obedience if we want to experience the glory of His life-giving power . . .

LOOK IN GOD'S WORD:

JOHN 11:38 Jesus, once more deeply moved, came to the tomb. It was a cave with a stone laid across the entrance.

³⁹"Take away the stone," he said. "But, Lord," said Martha, the sister of the dead man, "by this time there is a bad odor, for he has been there four days."

⁴⁰Then Jesus said, "Did I not tell you that if you believed, you would see the glory of God?"

⁴¹So they took away the stone. Then Jesus looked up and said, "Father, I thank you that you have heard me.

⁴²I knew that you always hear me, but I said this for the benefit of the people standing here, that they may believe that you sent me."

⁴³When he had said this, Jesus called in a loud voice, "Lazarus, come out!"

⁴⁴The dead man came out, his hands and feet wrapped with strips of linen, and a cloth around his face. Jesus said to them, "Take off the grave clothes and let him go."

LIST THE FACTS:

11:38 EXAMPLE: Jesus, deeply moved, came to the tomb.

LEARN THE LESSONS:

3 **11:38 EXAMPLE:** The death and burial of our loved ones is deeply moving to Jesus.

LISTEN TO HIS VOICE:

4 **11:38 EXAMPLE:** What am I doing to communicate the compassion of Jesus to those who are grieving?

5 LIVE IT OUT:

Pinpoint what God is saying to you from this passage. How will you respond? Write down today's date and what you will do now to live it out.

For additional insights on this passage, read *Just Give Me Jesus* pages 218–225.

Day Twenty-one

JOHN 18:1–11

Even Judas

Not only are we hopelessly doomed in our sin and guilt, not only did God the Father send His only Son to save us, not only did the Son give His life to do so, but we also shrugged off His sacrifice and said it wasn't necessary, boasting, "I can save myself by my own activity, or morality, or religiosity, or sincerity. I don't need a Savior."

We are oblivious to what God's Son did for us. We don't realize we need a Savior, much less have any gratitude for our salvation. But God demonstrated His love for us before we were even born by sending His Son to be our Savior. His Son is Jesus, Who makes sin forgivable for anyone. Even you. Even me. Even Judas . . .

LOOK IN GOD'S WORD:

JOHN 18:1 When he had finished praying, Jesus left with his disciples and crossed the Kidron Valley. On the other side there was an olive grove, and he and his disciples went into it.

²Now Judas, who betrayed him, knew the place, because Jesus had often met there with his disciples.

³So Judas came to the grove, guiding a detachment of soldiers and some officials from the chief priests and Pharisees. They were carrying torches, lanterns and weapons.

⁴Jesus, knowing all that was going to happen to him, went out and asked them, "Who is it you want?"

⁵"Jesus of Nazareth," they replied. "I am he," Jesus said. (And Judas the traitor was standing there with them.)

⁶When Jesus said, "I am he," they drew back and fell to the ground.

(Continued on page 120.)

LIST THE FACTS:

18:1 EXAMPLE: After He finished praying, Jesus crossed the Kidron Valley with His disciples.

3 **LEARN THE LESSONS:**

18:1 EXAMPLE: There is a time to pray and a time to act.

4 **LISTEN TO HIS VOICE:**

18:1 EXAMPLE: Do I know when to get off my knees and take action?

LOOK IN GOD'S WORD:

JOHN 18:7 Again he asked them, "Who is it you want?" And they said, "Jesus of Nazareth."

[8]"I told you that I am he," Jesus answered. "If you are looking for me, then let these men go."

[9]This happened so that the words he had spoken would be fulfilled: "I have not lost one of those you gave me."

[10]Then Simon Peter, who had a sword, drew it and struck the high priest's servant, cutting off his right ear. (The servant's name was Malchus.)

[11]Jesus commanded Peter, "Put your sword away! Shall I not drink the cup the Father has given me?"

LIST THE FACTS:

3 LEARN THE LESSONS:

4 LISTEN TO HIS VOICE:

5 LIVE IT OUT:

Pinpoint what God is saying to you from this passage. How will you respond? Write down today's date and what you will do now to live it out.

For additional insights on this passage, read *Just Give Me Jesus* pages 228–239.

Day Twenty-two

JOHN 18:12–18

Anyone Can Be Forgiven

Sometimes binding is in the will of God. Jesus was in the center of His Father's will, yet He was bound. He did not resist the tight cords or complain about His confinement. He simply submitted, not to the soldiers, but to His Father's will.

Jesus would have forgiven the very religious leaders who attacked Him if they had come humbly to Him and confessed their sins. In fact, Scripture indicates that two men, Joseph and Nicodemus, who were members of the Sanhedrin, did repent of their sins and receive forgiveness. Jesus makes sin forgivable for anyone—even those who attack Him . . .

LOOK IN GOD'S WORD:

JOHN 18:12 Then the detachment of soldiers with its commander and the Jewish officials arrested Jesus. They bound him

¹³and brought him first to Annas, who was the father-in-law of Caiaphas, the high priest that year.

¹⁴Caiaphas was the one who had advised the Jews that it would be good if one man died for the people.

¹⁵Simon Peter and another disciple were following Jesus. Because this disciple was known to the high priest, he went with Jesus into the high priest's courtyard,

¹⁶but Peter had to wait outside at the door. The other disciple, who was known to the high priest, came back, spoke to the girl on duty there and brought Peter in.

¹⁷"You are not one of his disciples, are you?" the girl at the door asked Peter. He replied, "I am not."

¹⁸It was cold, and the servants and officials stood around a fire they had made to keep warm. Peter also was standing with them, warming himself.

LIST THE FACTS:

18:12 EXAMPLE: The soldiers and Jewish officials arrested and bound Jesus.

LEARN THE LESSONS:

3 **18:12 EXAMPLE:** Sometimes the enemy's attack and our binding are within God's will and purpose for our lives.

LISTEN TO HIS VOICE:

4 **18:12 EXAMPLE:** In what way has God allowed me to be bound?

5 LIVE IT OUT:

Pinpoint what God is saying to you from this passage. How will you respond? Write down today's date and what you will do now to live it out.

For additional insights on this passage, read *Just Give Me Jesus* pages 239–244.

Day Twenty-three

JOHN 18:19–32

The Regret of a Lifetime

When Jesus was arrested in the garden, He expressly commanded the soldiers to let His disciples go, which they did. At the same time, He was also indirectly telling His disciples to leave. Nine of them obeyed while two of them did not. One, we assume, was John, a relative of the high priest, and the other was the loyal, bungling, impetuous Peter. They followed at a discreet distance as Jesus was led to the temple compound, which included the house of Annas, for His first religious trial. Then the disastrous drama that Peter would live to regret for the rest of his life began to unfold . . .

LOOK IN GOD'S WORD:

JOHN 18:19 Meanwhile, the high priest questioned Jesus about his disciples and his teaching.

²⁰"I have spoken openly to the world," Jesus replied. "I always taught in synagogues or at the temple, where all the Jews come together. I said nothing in secret.

²¹Why question me? Ask those who heard me. Surely they know what I said."

²²When Jesus said this, one of the officials nearby struck him in the face. "Is this the way you answer the high priest?" he demanded.

²³"If I said something wrong," Jesus replied, "testify as to what is wrong. But if I spoke the truth, why did you strike me?"

²⁴Then Annas sent him, still bound, to Caiaphas the high priest.

²⁵As Simon Peter stood warming himself, he was asked, "You are not one of his disciples, are you?" He denied it, saying, "I am not."

(Continued on page 130.)

LIST THE FACTS:

18:19 EXAMPLE: The priest questioned Jesus about His disciples and teaching.

LEARN THE LESSONS:

18:19 EXAMPLE: Oftentimes faultfinding with Christians and the Bible is rooted in antagonism toward Jesus.

LISTEN TO HIS VOICE:

18:19 EXAMPLE: What person or policy, official or organization is questioning the validity of the Bible and my credibility as a Christian?

LOOK IN GOD'S WORD:

JOHN 18:26 One of the high priest's servants, a relative of the man whose ear Peter had cut off, challenged him, "Didn't I see you with him in the olive grove?"

²⁷Again Peter denied it, and at that moment a rooster began to crow.

²⁸Then the Jews led Jesus from Caiaphas to the palace of the Roman governor. By now it was early morning, and to avoid ceremonial uncleanness the Jews did not enter the palace; they wanted to be able to eat the Passover.

²⁹So Pilate came out to them and asked, "What charges are you bringing against this man?"

³⁰"If he were not a criminal," they replied, "we would not have handed him over to you."

³¹Pilate said, "Take him yourselves and judge him by your own law." "But we have no right to execute anyone," the Jews objected.

³²This happened so that the words Jesus had spoken indicating the kind of death he was going to die would be fulfilled.

LIST THE FACTS:

3 **LEARN THE LESSONS:**

4 **LISTEN TO HIS VOICE:**

5 **LIVE IT OUT:**

Pinpoint what God is saying to you from this passage. How will you respond? Write down today's date and what you will do now to live it out.

For additional insights on this passage, read *Just Give Me Jesus* pages 245–249.

Day Twenty-four

JOHN 18:33–40

Dismissing the Truth

Pilate missed the opportunity of a lifetime—to ask the truth to explain Himself. Pilate had found the source of all Truth, the summation of all truth, the supremacy of all truth, yet he had casually dismissed Him as irrelevant! The Truth was staring him in the face, but Pilate wasn't interested. Pilate has many ideological children today who spend their lives and a lot of money searching for the truth while dismissing the gospel as irrelevant. The climate today, even within the church, can be so pragmatic, so political, so psychological, so philosophical, that we casually dismiss the Truth as an unnecessary complication to our plans and programs . . .

LOOK IN GOD'S WORD:

1

JOHN 18:33 Pilate then went back inside the palace, summoned Jesus and asked him, "Are you the king of the Jews?"

[34]"Is that your own idea," Jesus asked, "or did others talk to you about me?"

[35]"Am I a Jew?" Pilate replied. "It was your people and your chief priests who handed you over to me. What is it you have done?"

[36]Jesus said, "My kingdom is not of this world. If it were, my servants would fight to prevent my arrest by the Jews. But now my kingdom is from another place."

[37]"You are a king, then!" said Pilate. Jesus answered, "You are right in saying I am a king. In fact, for this reason I was born, and for this I came into the world, to testify to the truth. Everyone on the side of truth listens to me."

[38]"What is truth?" Pilate asked. With this he went out again to the Jews and said, "I find no basis for a charge against him.

[39]But it is your custom for me to release to you one prisoner at the time of the Passover. Do you want me to release 'the king of the Jews'?"

[40]They shouted back, "No, not him! Give us Barabbas!" Now Barabbas had taken part in a rebellion.

LIST THE FACTS:

2

18:33 EXAMPLE: Pilate summoned Jesus and asked, "Are you the king?"

LEARN THE LESSONS:

18:33 EXAMPLE: Even powerful and influential people are curious about Who Jesus really is.

LISTEN TO HIS VOICE:

18:33 EXAMPLE: What am I doing to give the truth about Jesus to those who are curious, regardless of who they might be?

5 LIVE IT OUT:

Pinpoint what God is saying to you from this passage. How will you respond? Write down today's date and what you will do now to live it out.

For additional insights on this passage, read *Just Give Me Jesus* pages 249–252.

Day Twenty-five

JOHN 19:1–16

There Is Still Hope

God remained silent in Herod's life because instead of repenting of his sin, "Herod and his soldiers ridiculed and mocked [Jesus]. Dressing Him in an elegant robe, they sent him back to Pilate." And once again, Pilate inwardly squirmed as he was confronted with making a decision about Jesus he had thought he could avoid.

And so Jesus, convicted of blasphemy by the religious courts but declared innocent of all charges by the Roman courts, was led off to be crucified. He was rejected by the religious leaders, by the Romans, and by His own people.

Whom do you know who is rejecting Jesus today? Whoever those people are, regardless of the vehemence of their words, or the hardness of their hearts, or the coldness of their eyes, there is still hope.

Look in God's Word:

JOHN 19:1 Then Pilate took Jesus and had him flogged.

²The soldiers twisted together a crown of thorns and put it on his head. They clothed him in a purple robe

³and went up to him again and again, saying, "Hail, king of the Jews!" And they struck him in the face.

⁴Once more Pilate came out and said to the Jews, "Look, I am bringing him out to you to let you know that I find no basis for a charge against him."

⁵When Jesus came out wearing the crown of thorns and the purple robe, Pilate said to them, "Here is the man!"

⁶As soon as the chief priests and their officials saw him, they shouted, "Crucify! Crucify!" But Pilate answered, "You take him and crucify him. As for me, I find no basis for a charge against him."

⁷The Jews insisted, "We have a law, and according to that law he must die, because he claimed to be the Son of God."

⁸When Pilate heard this, he was even more afraid,

⁹and he went back inside the palace. "Where do you come from?" he asked Jesus, but Jesus gave him no answer.

(Continued on page 140.)

List the Facts:

19:1 EXAMPLE: Pilate had Jesus flogged.

LEARN THE LESSONS:

3

19:1 EXAMPLE: Bad, cruel things happen to those God loves.

LISTEN TO HIS VOICE:

4

19:1 EXAMPLE: Why do I think my painful circumstances are a sign God doesn't love me?

1

LOOK IN GOD'S WORD:

John 19:10 "Do you refuse to speak to me?" Pilate said. "Don't you realize I have power either to free you or to crucify you?"

[11]Jesus answered, "You would have no power over me if it were not given to you from above. Therefore the one who handed me over to you is guilty of a greater sin."

[12]From then on, Pilate tried to set Jesus free, but the Jews kept shouting, "If you let this man go, you are no friend of Caesar. Anyone who claims to be a king opposes Caesar."

[13]When Pilate heard this, he brought Jesus out and sat down on the judge's seat at a place known as the Stone Pavement (which in Aramaic is Gabbatha).

[14]It was the day of Preparation of Passover Week, about the sixth hour. "Here is your king," Pilate said to the Jews.

[15]But they shouted, "Take him away! Take him away! Crucify him!" "Shall I crucify your king?" Pilate asked. "We have no king but Caesar," the chief priests answered.

[16]Finally Pilate handed him over to them to be crucified.

2

LIST THE FACTS:

3 **LEARN THE LESSONS:**

4 **LISTEN TO HIS VOICE:**

5 LIVE IT OUT:

Pinpoint what God is saying to you from this passage. How will you respond? Write down today's date and what you will do now to live it out.

For additional insights on this passage, read *Just Give Me Jesus* pages 252–261.

Day Twenty-six

JOHN 19:17–30

Forgiven!

The pervasive misconception today is that since Jesus died as a sacrifice for the sins of the world, then we are all automatically forgiven. But we overlook the vital truth that we must grasp the Lamb with our hands of faith and confess our sins. We then must acknowledge that He was slain for our sins as surely as if we had plunged the knife into His heart. At that moment, the Lamb becomes our High Priest and offers His own blood on the altar of the cross on our behalf. And, wonder of wonders! God accepts the sacrifice, and we are forgiven! Our guilt is atoned for! We are made right in God's sight! Jesus, the Lamb of God, makes sin forgivable for everyone . . . !

Look in God's Word:

John 19:17 Carrying his own cross, he went out to the place of the Skull (which in Aramaic is called Golgotha).

¹⁸Here they crucified him, and with him two others—one on each side and Jesus in the middle.

¹⁹Pilate had a notice prepared and fastened to the cross. It read: JESUS OF NAZARETH, THE KING OF THE JEWS.

²⁰Many of the Jews read this sign, for the place where Jesus was crucified was near the city, and the sign was written in Aramaic, Latin and Greek.

²¹The chief priests of the Jews protested to Pilate, "Do not write 'The King of the Jews,' but that this man claimed to be king of the Jews."

²²Pilate answered, "What I have written, I have written."

²³When the soldiers crucified Jesus, they took his clothes, dividing them into four shares, one for each of them, with the undergarment remaining. This garment was seamless, woven in one piece from top to bottom.

(Continued on page 146.)

List the Facts:

19:17 EXAMPLE: Jesus carried His own cross to Golgotha.

LEARN THE LESSONS:

3

19:17 EXAMPLE: Each of us is commanded to carry his or her own cross.

LISTEN TO HIS VOICE:

4

19:17 EXAMPLE: When have I deliberately taken up the cross of God's will for my life?

LOOK IN GOD'S WORD:

JOHN 19:24 "Let's not tear it," they said to one another. "Let's decide by lot who will get it." This happened that the scripture might be fulfilled which said, "They divided my garments among them and cast lots for my clothing." So this is what the soldiers did.

²⁵Near the cross of Jesus stood his mother, his mother's sister, Mary the wife of Clopas, and Mary Magdalene.

²⁶When Jesus saw his mother there, and the disciple whom he loved standing nearby, he said to his mother, "Dear woman, here is your son,"

²⁷and to the disciple, "Here is your mother." From that time on, this disciple took her into his home.

²⁸Later, knowing that all was now completed, and so that the Scripture would be fulfilled, Jesus said, "I am thirsty."

²⁹A jar of wine vinegar was there, so they soaked a sponge in it, put the sponge on a stalk of the hyssop plant, and lifted it to Jesus' lips.

³⁰When he had received the drink, Jesus said, "It is finished." With that, he bowed his head and gave up his spirit.

LIST THE FACTS:

3 **LEARN THE LESSONS:**

4 **LISTEN TO HIS VOICE:**

5 LIVE IT OUT:

Pinpoint what God is saying to you from this passage. How will you respond? Write down today's date and what you will do now to live it out.

For additional insights on this passage, read *Just Give Me Jesus* pages 262–283.

Day Twenty-seven

JOHN 19:38–20:9

Heaven Is Open!

After the long journey of life, we are going to look up and see heaven. We're going to hear voices lifted in songs of praise. We're going to see the glory of God radiating from within, and we're going to long for home. But we will be forbidden to enter. Heaven is closed to us because we are too dirty in our sin to enter it.

However, because Jesus found us in our hopeless, helpless state and offered us His hand at the cross, we can be welcomed into heaven. If we accept His offer and put our hand of faith in His, He will walk with us hand in hand, not only through the remainder of our journey, but through the gates of heaven that will be opened wide for us. We will be as welcomed and accepted in heaven as He is, solely because of our relationship and identification with Him. Praise God! Jesus is the One, and the only One, Who opens heaven to the sinner, not only through the cross, but also through His resurrection. Come and see the facts . . .

LOOK IN GOD'S WORD:

JOHN 19:38 Later, Joseph of Arimathea asked Pilate for the body of Jesus. Now Joseph was a disciple of Jesus, but secretly because he feared the Jews. With Pilate's permission, he came and took the body away.

³⁹He was accompanied by Nicodemus, the man who earlier had visited Jesus at night. Nicodemus brought a mixture of myrrh and aloes, about seventy-five pounds.

⁴⁰Taking Jesus' body, the two of them wrapped it, with the spices, in strips of linen. This was in accordance with Jewish burial customs.

⁴¹At the place where Jesus was crucified, there was a garden, and in the garden a new tomb, in which no one had ever been laid.

⁴²Because it was the Jewish day of Preparation and since the tomb was nearby, they laid Jesus there.

(Continued on page 152.)

LIST THE FACTS:

19:38 EXAMPLE: Joseph, a secret disciple, asked for and received permission from Pilate to take Jesus' body.

LEARN THE LESSONS:

19:38 EXAMPLE: The death of Jesus for us demands that we reject secrecy and openly, boldly identify with Him.

LISTEN TO HIS VOICE:

19:38 EXAMPLE: What excuse am I using for not publicly identifying with Jesus?

Look in God's Word:

JOHN 20:1 Early on the first day of the week, while it was still dark, Mary Magdalene went to the tomb and saw that the stone had been removed from the entrance.

²So she came running to Simon Peter and the other disciple, the one Jesus loved, and said, "They have taken the Lord out of the tomb, and we don't know where they have put him!"

³So Peter and the other disciple started for the tomb.

⁴Both were running, but the other disciple outran Peter and reached the tomb first.

⁵He bent over and looked in at the strips of linen lying there but did not go in.

⁶Then Simon Peter, who was behind him, arrived and went into the tomb. He saw the strips of linen lying there,

⁷as well as the burial cloth that had been around Jesus' head. The cloth was folded up by itself, separate from the linen.

⁸Finally the other disciple, who had reached the tomb first, also went inside. He saw and believed.

⁹(They still did not understand from Scripture that Jesus had to rise from the dead.)

List the Facts:

3 LEARN THE LESSONS:

4 LISTEN TO HIS VOICE:

5 LIVE IT OUT:

Pinpoint what God is saying to you from this passage. How will you respond? Write down today's date and what you will do now to live it out.

For additional insights on this passage, read *Just Give Me Jesus* pages 286–303.

Day Twenty-eight

JOHN 20:10–18

The Reason to Live

Mary Magdalene had been set free from her sin and her tormentors and her old self the day she met Jesus. Jesus had seen her—a person who was spiritually deformed and twisted by the enemy—yet He had looked past the obvious to the potential of the person she was meant to be. And He had loved her. For the first time in her life she had a reason for living. And He was her reason . . .

With His death, she had no peace and purpose in her life. She knew without Him she would never be anything other than what she had been—a desperate, hopeless, helpless, hell-bent sinner . . .

LOOK IN GOD'S WORD:

JOHN 20:10 Then the disciples went back to their homes,

¹¹but Mary stood outside the tomb crying. As she wept, she bent over to look into the tomb

¹²and saw two angels in white, seated where Jesus' body had been, one at the head and the other at the foot.

¹³They asked her, "Woman, why are you crying?" "They have taken my Lord away," she said, "and I don't know where they have put him."

¹⁴At this, she turned around and saw Jesus standing there, but she did not realize that it was Jesus.

¹⁵"Woman," he said, "why are you crying? Who is it you are looking for?" Thinking he was the gardener, she said, "Sir, if you have carried him away, tell me where you have put him, and I will get him."

¹⁶Jesus said to her, "Mary." She turned toward him and cried out in Aramaic, "Rabboni!" (which means Teacher).

¹⁷Jesus said, "Do not hold on to me, for I have not yet returned to the Father. Go instead to my brothers and tell them, 'I am returning to my Father and your Father, to my God and your God.'"

¹⁸Mary Magdalene went to the disciples with the news: "I have seen the Lord!" And she told them that he had said these things to her.

LIST THE FACTS:

20:10 EXAMPLE: The disciples went home.

LEARN THE LESSONS:

3

20:10 EXAMPLE: Often when we are confused, hurting, or grieving, we withdraw from others.

LISTEN TO HIS VOICE:

4

20:10 EXAMPLE: In my pain, how have I withdrawn from others?

5 LIVE IT OUT:

Pinpoint what God is saying to you from this passage. How will you respond? Write down today's date and what you will do now to live it out.

For additional insights on this passage, read *Just Give Me Jesus* pages 303–313.

Day Twenty-nine

JOHN 21:1–14

Failure Is Not Final

Peter was a failure. He had failed miserably to grasp the will of God when it was revealed to him, and he had brashly told Jesus He wasn't going to the cross. He had slept when he should have prayed, and he had almost provoked a massacre in the garden when he single-handedly tried to take on the Roman army and sliced off Malchus's ear. He had repeatedly sworn that even if all the other disciples forsook Jesus, he would die for Him—then he denied three times that very day that he even knew Him. There was no doubt in his mind or anyone else's that he was a miserable, habitual failure.

Do you feel like a failure? Have you been discouraged in your Christian life or your Christian leadership to the point of quitting? Do you feel you're just not cut out for this sort of thing? Then praise God! Failure is not final! He has a place for you in His kingdom because Jesus makes heaven available to the failure . . .

LOOK IN GOD'S WORD:

JOHN 21:1 Afterward Jesus appeared again to his disciples, by the Sea of Tiberias. It happened this way:

²Simon Peter, Thomas (called Didymus), Nathanael from Cana in Galilee, the sons of Zebedee, and two other disciples were together.

³"I'm going out to fish," Simon Peter told them, and they said, "We'll go with you." So they went out and got into the boat, but that night they caught nothing.

⁴Early in the morning, Jesus stood on the shore, but the disciples did not realize that it was Jesus.

⁵He called out to them, "Friends, haven't you any fish?" "No," they answered.

⁶He said, "Throw your net on the right side of the boat and you will find some." When they did, they were unable to haul the net in because of the large number of fish.

⁷Then the disciple whom Jesus loved said to Peter, "It is the Lord!" As soon as Simon Peter heard him say, "It is the Lord," he wrapped his outer garment around him (for he had taken it off) and jumped into the water.

(Continued on page 162.)

LIST THE FACTS:

21:1 EXAMPLE: Jesus appeared again to His disciples.

LEARN THE LESSONS:

3

21:1 EXAMPLE: Jesus will not leave us alone.

LISTEN TO HIS VOICE:

4

21:1 EXAMPLE: In what way have I experienced the comforting presence of Jesus—again?

1 LOOK IN GOD'S WORD:

JOHN 21:8 The other disciples followed in the boat, towing the net full of fish, for they were not far from shore, about a hundred yards.

⁹When they landed, they saw a fire of burning coals there with fish on it, and some bread.

¹⁰Jesus said to them, "Bring some of the fish you have just caught."

¹¹Simon Peter climbed aboard and dragged the net ashore. It was full of large fish, 153, but even with so many the net was not torn.

¹²Jesus said to them, "Come and have breakfast." None of the disciples dared ask him, "Who are you?" They knew it was the Lord.

¹³Jesus came, took the bread and gave it to them, and did the same with the fish.

¹⁴This was now the third time Jesus appeared to his disciples after he was raised from the dead.

2 LIST THE FACTS:

3 **LEARN THE LESSONS:**

4 **LISTEN TO HIS VOICE:**

5 Live It Out:

Pinpoint what God is saying to you from this passage. How will you respond? Write down today's date and what you will do now to live it out.

For additional insights on this passage, read *Just Give Me Jesus* pages 314–327.

Day Thirty

JOHN 21:15–25

Do You Love Jesus?

Jesus looked straight at Peter without glancing at anyone or anything else and asked persistently for the third time, "Simon son of John, do you love me?" Under the direct, searching gaze of his Lord, Peter must have known he was being asked whether he loved Jesus more than himself. This time did Peter squirm uncomfortably? Did he love Jesus more than the opinions of others, such as the servant girl in the courtyard? More than his own safety and comfort, as he would not be dangerously identified with Someone Who had been executed as an enemy of Rome? More than his own reputation? More than his memories of sin and failure?

Do *you* love Jesus . . . ?

LOOK IN GOD'S WORD:

JOHN 21:15 When they had finished eating, Jesus said to Simon Peter, "Simon son of John, do you truly love me more than these?" "Yes, Lord," he said, "you know that I love you." Jesus said, "Feed my lambs."

¹⁶Again Jesus said, "Simon son of John, do you truly love me?" He answered, "Yes, Lord, you know that I love you." Jesus said, "Take care of my sheep."

¹⁷The third time he said to him, "Simon son of John, do you love me?" Peter was hurt because Jesus asked him the third time, "Do you love me?" He said, "Lord, you know all things; you know that I love you." Jesus said, "Feed my sheep.

¹⁸I tell you the truth, when you were younger you dressed yourself and went where you wanted; but when you are old you will stretch out your hands, and someone else will dress you and lead you where you do not want to go."

¹⁹Jesus said this to indicate the kind of death by which Peter would glorify God. Then he said to him, "Follow me!"

(Continued on page 168.)

LIST THE FACTS:

21:15 EXAMPLE: When they finished eating, Jesus asked, "Simon, do you love Me?"

LEARN THE LESSONS:

21:15 EXAMPLE: Immediately after mealtimes can be an ideal time for family devotions and discussion of spiritual things.

LISTEN TO HIS VOICE:

21:15 EXAMPLE: How has this devotional journal caused me to love Jesus more?

LOOK IN GOD'S WORD:

JOHN 21:20 Peter turned and saw that the disciple whom Jesus loved was following them. (This was the one who had leaned back against Jesus at the supper and had said, "Lord, who is going to betray you?")

²¹When Peter saw him, he asked, "Lord, what about him?"

²²Jesus answered, "If I want him to remain alive until I return, what is that to you? You must follow me."

²³Because of this, the rumor spread among the brothers that this disciple would not die. But Jesus did not say that he would not die; he only said, "If I want him to remain alive until I return, what is that to you?"

²⁴This is the disciple who testifies to these things and who wrote them down. We know that his testimony is true.

²⁵Jesus did many other things as well. If every one of them were written down, I suppose that even the whole world would not have room for the books that would be written.

LIST THE FACTS:

3 **LEARN THE LESSONS:**

4 **LISTEN TO HIS VOICE:**

5 Live It Out:

Pinpoint what God is saying to you from this passage. How will you respond? Write down today's date and what you will do now to live it out.

For additional insights on this passage, read *Just Give Me Jesus* pages 327–342.

Also Available from Anne Graham Lotz

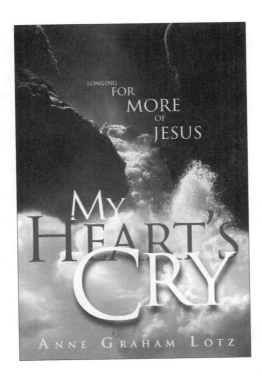

MY HEART'S CRY

Anne Graham Lotz delivers a powerful message on our longing to know Jesus more intimately, based on the Savior's last days with His disciples as recorded in the Gospel of John.

Long heralded by Billy Graham as the "best preacher in the family," Anne Graham Lotz draws new insights from passages containing Jesus' teachings to his disciples toward the end of his earthly ministry when the disciples were trying to cling to Him most. Anne writes, "I wanted to know what He had to say to those who were desperate for more of Him."

Also available on audio cassette.

W PUBLISHING GROUP™

www.wpublishinggroup.com

Also Available from Anne Graham Lotz

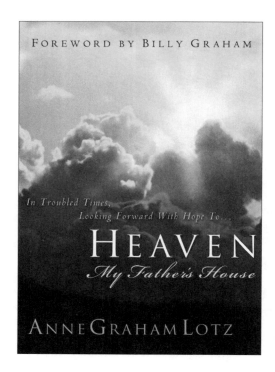

HEAVEN: MY FATHER'S HOUSE

Jesus promised us, "In My Father's house are many rooms...I am going there to prepare a place for you." Amid the turbulence of today's terror-besieged world, we cling to the hope of a heavenly home where we will be welcomed into eternal peace and safety. Anne affirms that Heaven is the home of your dreams: a home of lasting value that's fully paid for and filled with family, where you will be wanted and welcomed. Best of all, Heaven is a home you are invited to claim as your own.

Also available on DVD and audio cassette.

W PUBLISHING GROUP™

www.wpublishinggroup.com

Also Available from Anne Graham Lotz

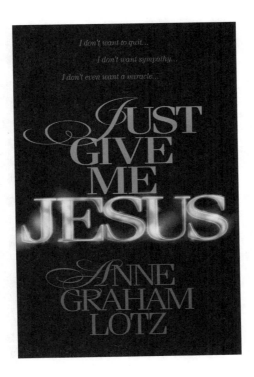

JUST GIVE ME JESUS

Learn from Anne Graham Lotz' heart cry: I don't want to quit, I don't want sympathy, I don't even want a miracle, just give me Jesus!

After two pressure-filled, life-changing years of professional exhaustion and personal turmoil, Anne Graham Lotz found herself with only one heart-cry, "Please, just give me Jesus." In this faith-inspiring book, she stares intently at the realities of life with her Savior. To those needing a fresh start, to those still searching for happiness, to those in need of forgiveness, to the suffering and the self-righteous alike, Jesus was, is, and will always be the answer.

W Publishing Group™

www.wpublishinggroup.com

Also Available from Anne Graham Lotz

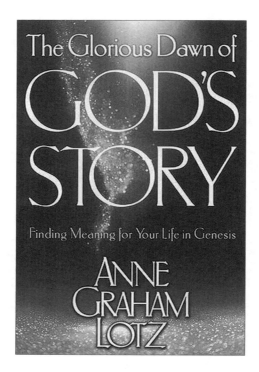

GOD'S STORY

Anne Graham Lotz leads you through the first eleven chapters of Genesis, unlocking hidden messages in the familiar stories of Creation, Adam and Eve, Cain and Abel, Noah and the ark, the Tower of Babel, and others. She thoughtfully illuminates each moment of Creation with inspiring insights and probing reflections to better reveal God, the Creator of us all. In *God's Story* you will thrill to the beauty, majesty, and tenderness of God's personal involvement in creating the world, and you will come to recognize the Creator's infinite power at work in your life as well.

W PUBLISHING GROUP™

www.wpublishinggroup.com

Also Available from Anne Graham Lotz

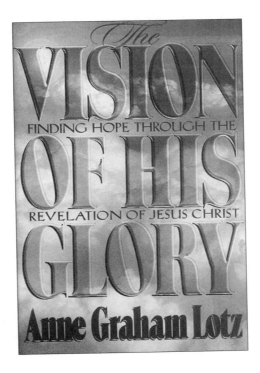

THE VISION OF HIS GLORY

With an inspiring sense of wonder and a focus on Jesus Christ, Anne Graham Lotz brings clarity and understanding to the book of Revelation. Lotz takes the reader step-by-step through John's eyewitness account of God's plan for our future, emphasizing our hope in Jesus rather than our fear of end times

W PUBLISHING GROUP™

www.wpublishinggroup.com